The Ring of Moss

ANTHONY KINGSMILL-LUNN

ANN RIVERS

BETTINA HELEN MASSIE

RICHARD MAELZEL-MARTINS

ALEX CURZON HALE

IMELDA KEYEN

DONALD MACLEOD

An environmentally friendly book printed and bound in England by
www.printondemand-worldwide.com

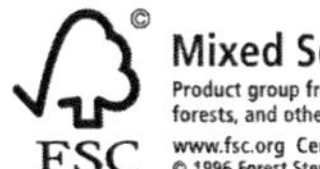

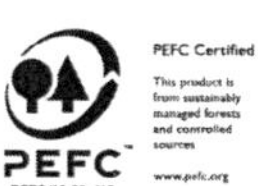

This book is made entirely of chain-of-custody materials

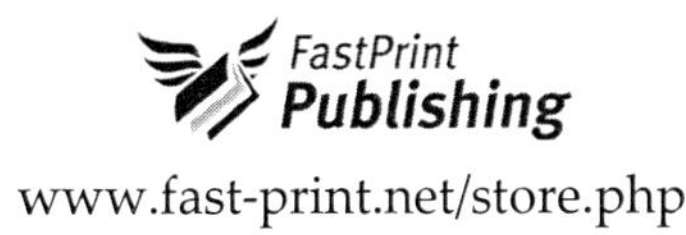

www.fast-print.net/store.php

The Ring of Moss

ISBN 978-178035-436-1

First published 2013 by
FASTPRINT PUBLISHING
Peterborough, England.

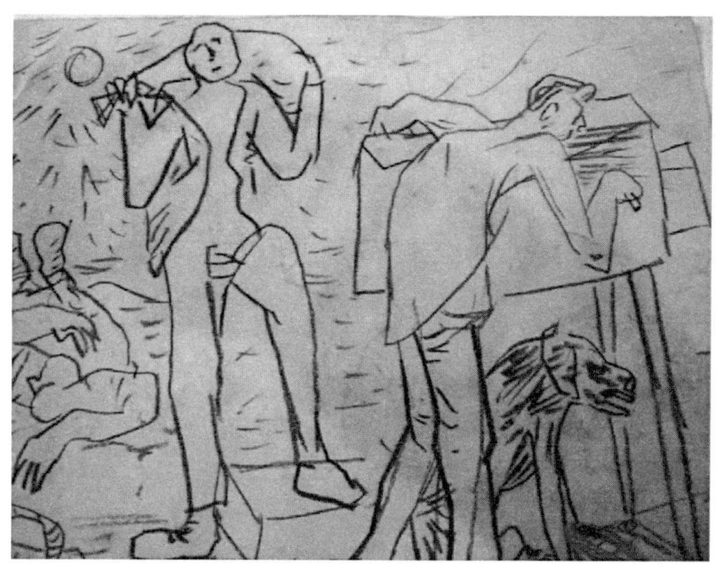

Anthony Kingsmill *A day in the field with dog*

The Ring of Moss

When I was ten years old my parents lived in a house on the rise of a hill beside playing fields in a district known as Red Lake, so called because of the Battle of Senlac which was fought nearby during the Battle of Hastings. The place we lived in then was an old mill which had been converted into a house, and a crude attempt had been made to combine a Tudor atmosphere inside with that of the mill itself. The banisters were of rope and the electric lights shone through leaded lanterns, the kind one associates with certain Merry Christmas cards. The windows were leaded cross-wise, and only the ceilings with their dark oak beams preserved what was genuine of the original old mill. The house was known as the Black Mill, as its outside was covered by black tar paint. It was a square compact house with a red roof, and from the dining room French windows opened out onto a crazy-paved yard with a bird bath plonked in the middle. A tall hedge separated us from neighbours on one side and a small path led from the yard to an unkempt lawn with small stumpy trees, that in time would make a miniature orchard. A hedge from this garden separated us from the playing fields and whoever happened to be in the garden was often summoned to throw back a cricket or football by a plaintive call from the other side of the hedge. Our house had the reputation for being haunted, perhaps because it was often unoccupied, and speaking for myself that time was haunted by melancholy impressions. My parents quarrelled there a great deal and I was very much out of favour. I spent as much time as I could away from the house, my brother and sister being too young to follow me and share my adventures with poorer and wilder children of the district.

We did not live there more than a year and a half but it was during this time I was sent to the grammar School at Hastings, which from our district was two miles away down a steep hill in the town by the sea. I tried to make up for the lack of attention at home by showing off, asserting myself and generally misbehaving in front of my school mates - so that I was frequently punished, both at school and at home, for being a nuisance. My stepfather would call me up to his study and that sinking feeling I had when I crept up the staircase clutching the rope banister to stand before him and touch my toes became a familiar experience.

At that time I became attached to a boy much older than myself who befriended me, partly to get to know my stepfather who was quite a literary figure in Hastings. This friend would take me for long walks, and I remember that with him these walks invariably led us inland away from the sea towards a sloping ridge which, seen from a distance, appeared perpetually covered in a white frost, but on nearer view became a large cemetery with marble graves and crosses. He was ill-fed and pale and although only seventeen I never thought of him as young. On these walks he would tell me frightful ghost stories with such details of supernatural horror that the landscape around me as I listened would grow sinister and strange, as though something hidden in the soil itself was corrupting the country fields and lanes. These stories and my uneasy life at home combined to form a particular impression of that time, so that for many years after I dreamt I was back at the Black Mill with a sense of foreboding, peering through the leaded windows at those rooms tenanted by memories and shadows that enveloped the house and its black crown of tar.

My stepfather was not a successful writer in the worldly sense. He was a man of letters with a vast love and knowledge of literature, but he offended many of his contemporaries by his judgements and was more or less neglected by them. His exposure of their false prophets did not meet with their approval, and his finer gifts of perception were equally cold-shouldered. He suffered considerably from this neglect, which brought out sometimes the bullying and tyrannical side of his nature, but it never dimmed his zest and humour for debunking what he considered ridiculous and vain. His father was a Victorian who had made a lot of money by building hotels in Switzerland at the time when winter sports were becoming fashionable. By inviting the higher clergy over for free holidays, which were gladly accepted, he ensured the success of this venture, and his hotels were soon filled by the wealthy classes whose upbringing had thrived on the strenuous Puritanism of English Public Schools. God and Manor thus reconciled, he was knighted for his services to the church and Empire, and his business thrived. My stepfather was sent to Harrow and served in his father's business for a while after the first world war, but the urge to be free and write precipitated a quarrel with his parents that was to bruise him spiritually and lame him financially. Somewhere along the line his teeth had been set on edge and what was romantic and idealistic in his nature conflicted with a hard core of puritanism at the roots of his being that I am certain was responsible for his occasional terrible rages and his habit of using the stick like a tyrannical headmaster, so that I loved and hated him with alternate intensity.

I remember as a child of four when he first became my stepfather, he would play a game with me in which he was a great giant striding towards me over the carpet in seven league boots and the only way I could stop him was to let out a magic whistle and I was saved. The game was very real and in terror, half of fear at not being able to whistle, and of his fearsomely comic appearance with his hunched shoulders and red face, I would burst into excited laughter and desperately try to shape my lips and force out the necessary sound before he reached me.

I often think that image of him was true during our Black Mill period - only it seemed I had forgotten the magic formula and it was no longer a game. But yet I loved him when on other occasions he would change from a seven leagued monster into the friendliest giant on earth and lift me on his shoulders to share his delight and wonder at the world spread before him.

The period covering our life at the Black Mill was marked by my mother's return from Germany where she had been to stay with a well known Teacher and philosopher. I must explain that before we came to the Black Mill, my stepfather five years before had dumped us as a family in a small provincial town on the shores of Lake Geneva. He came over for brief visits only, and my mother during this phase was decidedly unhappy. She felt very cut off and miserable and I don't know to this day what made him do this, but he was to suffer for it later. She had built up strong reserves of resentment and by the time we were brought back to England - his two children by their marriage my half sister and baby brother and myself - her mind was made up and I think it was from this stage that dissolution within the family framework set in and she began consciously to turn away from him and satisfy her frustrated soul by focusing her attention on another great Figure who would redeem and point the way to self discovery. It was then we moved to the Black Mill.

On the return from Germany she had changed indeed. Her migraines intensified and her temper became formidable. They quarrelled a great deal and as the only child of her unhappy first marriage I suffered in a different way to my stepsister and brother, as I was more strongly attached to my mother than they since their love was linked by organic ties to both a father and a mother. For my stepfather this was a difficult time. I think he was feeling guilty towards my mother and trying to make up for it, but by then it was too late, and although he did not die till 1948 a part of him began to die at the Black Mill. My mother continually reproached him for spending too much time and energy on his friends and I remember her set face as his burst of laughter reverberated through the house as he indulged in telephone conversations that lasted an hour and a half. He began writing parodies with writer friends which helped financially and afforded him the opportunity to leave the domestic set up and go away on travelling jaunts, on holidays with the muses, to happy highlands in the footsteps of Johnson and Boswell, or with another he would set off and rediscover in London the England of Elizabeth and Shakespeare and that teeming past would live again as they heard Falstaff echo their laughter through the glades.

In 1946 I married against the wishes of my mother and stepfather. By this time he was a tired man and developed a serious stomach complaint, so that a great deal of the following year was spent in hospital. He had two operations which did not cure him, and I know by this time he wanted to let go of life. A few days before his death I had a strange dream. I was standing in the hallway of the Black Mill a few yards from the front door which was closed. It was night and the electric light was on with its inevitable lantern covering. Suddenly a violent gust of wind blew open the front door, and standing there framed in the doorway against the wild darkness outside I saw my stepfather dressed in black evening clothes, with cloak and top hat. He seemed charged with a tense energy by the suddenness of his visitation and though in essence I seemed to stand before him, he looked past me and shouted a loud and imperative HALLO. It was as though he was demanding attention, not in hope of a familiar response, but directed at a void that engaged his whole being, that would answer him, though he was waiting. I woke immediately with that "hallo" as though a gong had been struck inside me, and as I lay there frightened I began to imagine he was now really dying and had come to tell me so.

Some time before I had this dream he had come out of the hospital, and he and my mother were staying in a cottage they had rented near Steyning, close by the Downs and a few miles from Brighton. It was not a large cottage but had a thatched roof and was oak beamed and pleasant. By this time my wife had been grudgingly accepted as one of the family and we both went down to spend a weekend with them. I remember the visit particularly, as it was the last time I saw him in a natural setting, the next visit to see him being in the hospital where he was dying. I had become, since my marriage, argumentative with him for several reasons. In the first place he never forgave my wife for our marriage and deep down neither did I, which I unfairly took out on him; but also a form of disillusion had set its claws in me.

My stepfather was fond of an Elizabethan quotation "The High Hill of the Muses, Always Calm and Clear". The war and marriage had broken up for me my felicity in this belief, also I saw him unjustly compromised and weak where he should have been strong, and I was either not mature enough, or too emotionally involved with him, to forgive the past for myself and for him. I left home at the age of 14 and had sleepwalked my way into 16, when suddenly out of the blue I was granted a vision of Joy and Bliss, as I drank of the fountain of Light. "Trees were green, mountains sheer, And God dramatically clear." Poetry enhanced the revelation, and I went home on brief visits.

I was never so close to my stepfather as then. We would quote back to each other, and feel the bond that binds those who drink from the same source. But the war numbed a part of me, and marriage likewise. I turned to the poets whose season in Hell corresponded more closely to my state of mind, rather than to those who sang on the fields of praise! I was at enmity with Joy and hid Wordsworth in a suitcase under the bed. I pained my stepfather and I will always feel sad that I wanted him to realise this at the time I should have loved and been more gentle.

This time then, on my last visit, I remember sitting on the lawn by the cottage near my mother, who was resting in a deckchair. Even in sleep, she lacked a quality of repose and unity, and I remember noticing that some shadows cast from branches nearly fell across her body, complicating and distorting the image I had of her so that shadows and body and deckchair created an unequal insect-like appearance at odds with the peace and natural setting of garden and trees. At that moment, from the house, the red face of my stepfather appeared at the window about to put on a green pullover. There was a glimpse of the jersey being pulled over the head, but it had a tight roll-necked collar and I could hear muffled curses and heavy breathing, until suddenly this flushed face appeared laughing as it broke through and I saw the friendly giant again with the magic mantle of nature on him, almost too big for the sugar loaf house but so much part of the setting that were he not there the heart of it all would be missing.

Soon after the dream, my mother phoned me to say he was critically ill in hospital again and this time there was little hope. We arranged to meet in Brighton and she would take my wife to the hospital. We both felt forlorn and lost as we sat in the train, it was a grey late August day and as we approached our destination we could see the gloomy backs of the

Downs. My mother was calm and collected and we began our walk towards the hospital. We did not talk much, but an odd coincidence drew our attention to a particular shop window that displayed a life-size dummy sitting in a chair. It was fully dressed and its face very pink with that blank bright look that ventriloquist dummies have. As we drew near the shop it began to rock slowly backwards and forwards, as though it were laughing but not a sound came from it, only movement. We watched it dumbly as it gathered strength and shook itself about, and its motions became more violent. The hands began to slap the knees in time with its opening and closing eyes and jaw, until a final paroxysm of jerks slumped it and brought it to a stop.

We giggled nervously and walked on by an almost deserted sea front and its trellised shelters. The esplanade seemed to stretch for miles and on the beach I could only see a lonely figure of a man throwing stones into the water, with a dog barking beside him unwilling to follow the stone thrown by its master. We began to climb up the sloping part of the front and looking down I could see a children's funfair and miniature railway. The engines and other machinery were wrapped up for the winter and the railway lines looked unused and rusted. The sea was sullen and the elaborate pier needed freshening up.

We turned our backs to the sea and walking up the steep road arrived at the hospital. The smell of disinfectant and anaesthetic as usual pervaded the atmosphere and the people generally rushing about. Such places are a kind of transit camp in a shadow land between sickness and health, and I always have to fight off thoughts of actual physical pain and operations whenever I visit.

We went up in a lift and were shown into a ward. As I came into the room I saw a group of people standing round a bed in which a man was wrapped up. The light of the window near him fell on his head, which was skull-like and luminous with the disease that was ravaging him, and my mother later told me he had died a few hours after. My stepfather was halfway up the ward and terribly changed. His face lit up as he saw us and he said he was much happier since they had moved him from the ground floor, as there he had faced a window that looked out onto a blank wall, but now he could see a rooftop and the sky and imagine the sea not far away.

I struggled to control my tears and he held out his arms and embraced me; he began to tell my mother a dream he had the night before, in which he had seen Christ on a cross in the middle of the ward and as he looked it had suddenly turned into a pillar of fire.

Even then I heard my mother giving him her interpretation of his anguish.

If it calmed him I do not know, but it seemed to me she was hammering in the last nails of his coffin. As her will gathered strength and grew more terrible as it was denied, she had turned to Theosophy and analysis and began to assume a saviour role which she bludgeoned him with, as his desire to let go of life became more and more apparent, and now again she was trying to tidy up the damage by persuading herself his illness was the result of unsolved Freudian problems, which she over the last few years had been trying to make him face. In this there was a great deal of ignorance on her part, but I also believe a lot of conscious destructive will, but this time he was leaving for good and it did not matter anymore.

Two days later he died. I was not there but my sister told me he did not have to struggle to leave this world.

I went down with my wife once more to stay at the cottage in order to attend his cremation. My mother did not seem grief stricken, and from that time onwards I began to observe her with a curious detachment. In a way through my stepfather's death she had ceased to exist for me really as a mother. Something in me had snapped, and I felt I was drifting out to sea, but to where I could not tell. I felt empty and lost.

The day before the funeral my mother told me I must go and see my stepfather at the undertaker, mysteriously adding it would help me. I did not really want to, but had no wish to offend her and I set off on my own that afternoon. It was a three or four mile walk to the outskirts of Steyning. My mind was a blank, and in a mood of listless curiosity I noticed after walking half an hour I had reached a barn-like building set back from the road with a notice nailed on the gate "Cat Museum" entrance 6d. I decided to go in and paid my sixpence to an old crone in a shawl, the image I thought of a witch in Hansel and Gretel, who pokes children in the oven to see if they are fattening up nicely. The barn was full of dusty glass cases displaying groups of stuffed kittens. The first case I examined had a kitten football match and each one was dressed for the occasion in football shirt, shorts and boots. There was even a referee blowing the whistle, the match taking place on a papier mache field with miniature goalposts at each end of the case. An attempt at realism had been achieved by the creator of this strange fantasy, for at on end the pussy goalkeeper leaned against his goalpost, paws crossed as his team was doing well at the other end of the field. The next case was a cricket match. There was a pavilion with the clock set at

3.37. This spectacle was more hideous than the last in that their little flannels were faded and yellow with age. The wicket keeper crouched behind the match-sized wicket and the tiny cricket bat had just hit the red bead of a ball. This time they wore caps. The barn included an orchestra, a hunting scene, a painter in nineteenth century beret and flowing cravat with his model on a throne with its fur intact, and a section devoted to various accidents of nature: three-headed, five- footed, two-tailed monsters and a few shapes in bottles I did not wish to examine closely.

I came out dazed into the light and the road, feeling rather sick. Soon after I reached the undertakers and waited in his front parlour. A mild middle aged man with a bald head came and shook hands with me gently and explained that the deceased was in a shed at the back garden and would I follow him.

We walked up the patch beside his vegetable patch and reaching the shed walked in. The coffin lay in the middle of the shed on a table, and not quite knowing what to do I went over without realising I been building up a picture of my stepfather lying in state in the stillness of his death, that I had hoped would clarify the confusion of my thoughts when I should have to face him thus, and the mystery of his final sleep would imprint on my heart a sorrowful acceptance of the sadness I would feel in the loss. In truth I could not really believe he was dead, and when I looked into the coffin I was taken by surprise by what I felt was a dreadful sham. My stepfather presented a terrible parody of all I had previously imagined. His face had shrunk considerably and around it was a Victorian lace sleeping bonnet. He looked absurd and irritable, pinched and mean, and chalky deposits of white dust like badly applied powder lay round the crevices and dips of his features, the result of a plaster death mask my mother insisted she would have.

The undertaker hovered near me and told me gently to touch the body explaining that if I did, the image before me would be laid forever and would not harass my dreams.

I bent down and put my lips onto his brow avoiding the lace edge of the bonnet. I had often kissed him so as a child, remembering the salt taste on my lips as he said "Good night old man", but this time the coldness of that surface made me realise it was the most one-sided kiss of all my life. I came out into the street and began to walk very fast, following a side turning that would lead me onto a path that led to the Downs. I reached the end of the houses and started up the winding path. After an hour climbing I stopped and turned back to look. The plain I had left was beginning to level out below me and I tried to whip up a sense of belonging to the landscape by quoting some lines that I loved myself, but I knew I was shamming. The weather was uncertain and the plain appeared to brood in itself and not let any associations free, and the postcard sized houses in the distance looked blank and anonymous, with the fields and rows of trees stretching away to a vague fuzz of no definable horizon. The bushes began thinning out, and on the white chalky path, which was beginning to narrow, I could see the stale dry pellets of sheep dropping, but no shepherd with his flock was visible, and I had not seen a soul since I left the houses of the town. I decided I would make for the ring which I could see ahead like a dark mole on the brow of the hill. I was isolated and beginning to tire, and felt like a beetle crawling over some tremendous monolith. At last I reached the summit of the hill and the ring was only four or five hundred yards away. The path petered out to a stop and I found myself walking on a flat level of fine moss-like grass. Between the trees of the ring the recesses looked dark and uninviting and I began to imagine the ancients there in their long white beards performing strange rites and ceremonies, and that in those dark ages someone such as I had stood this same mossy ground perhaps as sacrificial victim and on this very spot experienced his first sharp pang of fear and doubt. I had a feeling of wanting to take off my shoes and socks but resisted it. A kind of excitement that was vaguely apprehensive began to stir in me, and walking quickly towards the ring I reached a ditch which encircled it, jumped over and in a moment was inside the ring amongst the trees. The light was dim and ghostly and the strong smell of rotting leaves and intense silence created a gloomy oppressive atmosphere. I became uneasy, and started as I broke the silence by treading on a twig, becoming very conscious of myself and felt as if I was being watched by unseen presences from the dark corners of the bushes and the trees. My bowels suddenly felt a heat in them and a violent urge to abandon myself and scatter my seed on the ground possessed me, as an offering to Eros in this dark shrine on the thighs of the hills. But a superstitious fear or higher will prevented me and I crept out of the forest and into the ditch outside the ring and, pulling down my trousers, I satisfied a more natural need as though consciously I was also expelling from my system the grieves and sorrows of the foregoing days. Then an impulse directed me to the centre of the ring again, and kneeling down I prayed to the Holy Spirit of this Temple to watch over me and grant me courage to fulfil my destiny. Once more I left the ring and began to run down the slopes of the hill with a sense of freedom and exultation, and on reaching the level fields and lanes looked back for the last time at the black lump of the ring, now almost swallowed by the dark mass of the hills, and it seemed to me that a part of my past was vanishing with it and only the dark skyline of the hills stood clear as an emblem of the future to which I was pledged.

The next day the service was carried out in the crematorium, situated in the outskirts of Brighton. We sat in a pew in front of a raised stage with dark violet curtains drawn aside to show the coffin laid on a trolley. The burial service was read, and when it was over a hidden gramophone began to play Handel's Largo. The curtains the colour of night began slowly to draw together, and the coffin slid away from us and vanished. As the curtains finally touched, it seemed I was witnessing the close of a solemn play whose meaning I had not fully grasped, but that somewhere in the shadows of the wings lay the answer which only love itself would reveal.

END

In memory of Hugh Kingsmill

Anthony Kingsmill-Lunn

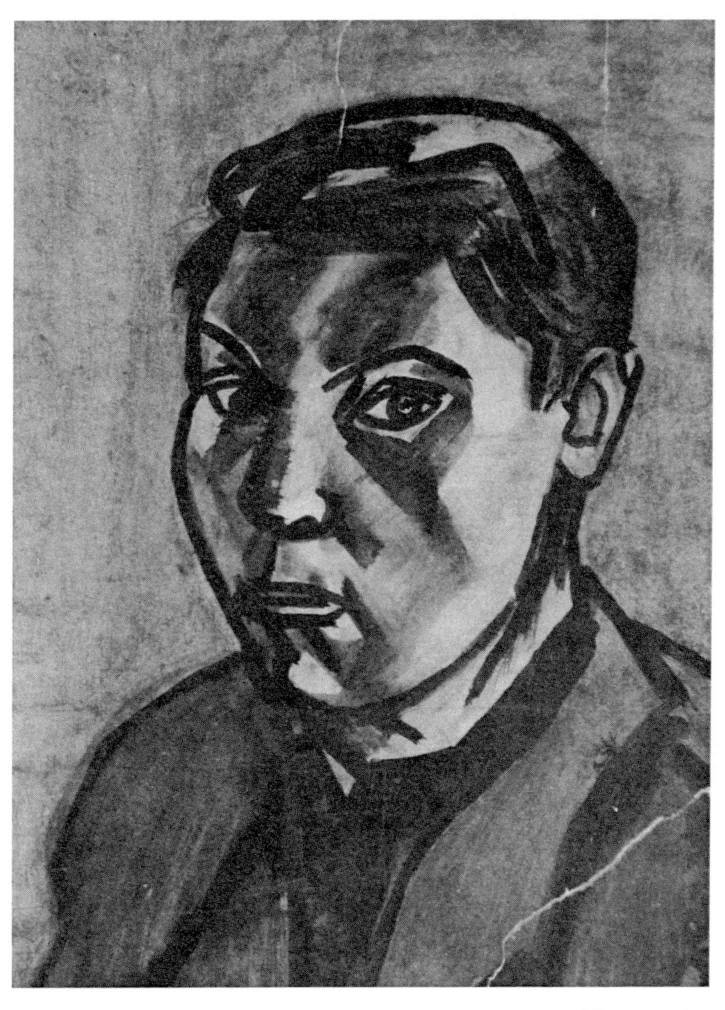

Anthony Kingsmill *Self Portrait*

Return To Theseus, Greece And The Dawn Of Legend

Long before Homer, Sophocles and Ezra Pound
You went forth into the gold Sophoclean light
and bore your wounds gladly.
As the clear stream of the water tumbling over the rocks
flows down the gorge between the two great hills
and falls gently into the sacred grove
upon those hills as a boy, leaping over rocks
you stalked your prey hungry for Destiny and legend.
So starving wide awake
until you lifted up the heavy stone
knowing at last what you must do.
The sandals fit, your father's word belongs to you.
Driven by your will and the birth of Legend
the triumph, the fury of your call
from that great stone to the palace walls
was heard and echoed in the hills.
Another age, another dawn, blind Homer listening
heard the echo and sang it to another Word
Who can deny the Word…
And time that is eternal as dew and new ploughed earth
is Man's destiny in furrows of silvering light:

We bathe in your clear waters to hope we are baptised
more courage to leap over walls
The will to obey the act
the act to sing the word
All lesser poets follow and sing to keep the word
Among these rocks so still in shade and filtered light,
so still in your sacred pool
We are ghosts returning to haunt as blue-winged
dragonflies hovering over these rocks
our reflections darting over water
and wind fallen lemons from their trees
the bitter fruit of memory in time
lie scattered, half hidden in the grassy banks
We have to return again…
We are amazed and call to Ariadne
Abandoned on Naxos and her unquiet sands,
a thread a thread
leads us out of this maze towards the waiting poem
We have slain our Minotaurs in walking dreams,
we have crossed dry river beds.
Prometheus the sun lights up every day
Attica is waiting for destiny
Bull of Minos, over your golden crescent horns,
time somersaults ..the dance is still the dream of Man.

Anthony Kingsmill-Lunn

Poros and Trizinia 22nd June 1987

The Cracker Factory

Help Help! I am a prisoner
In a Chinese cracker factory
This is the year of the Dragon
Remember Remember, the 5th of November
I'll be there
I appeared with the Chinese
Some time ago, who imagined
How foolishly, they could avoid War
By having me around.
Meanwhile
They had delicious fun with cooking and torture and one bad
Tempered Emperor in a tantrum
Swallowed a ton of gold leaf
cause I got wet before the party
This all by the way.
The trouble is
I have been used for Money
gang warfare and seen the massacre of Innocents
They use me in Literature in rather
obvious ways.

Anthony Kingsmill-Lunn

Hydra, 22nd May 1987

For All Of Us Sitting Still

Lord I pray
Forgive my fear, the fear of vanity; and vanity itself.
Not to be afraid of what is your will.
In joy and sorrow.
And please, please Lord
Preserve me from self pity and bow
and violin strings before the mirror.
Not to jump blindly over cliffs
or too far lead astray.
Even pigs with hairy snout
Protest against the use of pearls;
Politically they are right
Your prodigal Son was tamed by them
And will always come back to you.

Anthony Kingsmill-Lunn

Hydra 2nd June 1987

For Juan Gris

Remembering your signature
In the frozen frame of art
I see you as a child
engined at first
Cartoons to follow, the media,
yet you still apart
Waiting for surrender
into your cubist heart
Sentimental always, severe as
a target waiting for a dart
I tried to imitate you
your last painting
your adieu to the Muses and to Art.
More baroque as you were leaving
the engineering gone
Your Pierrot head averted
Hands folded
Hugging a green guitar.

Anthony Kingsmill-Lunn

Hydra, June 1987

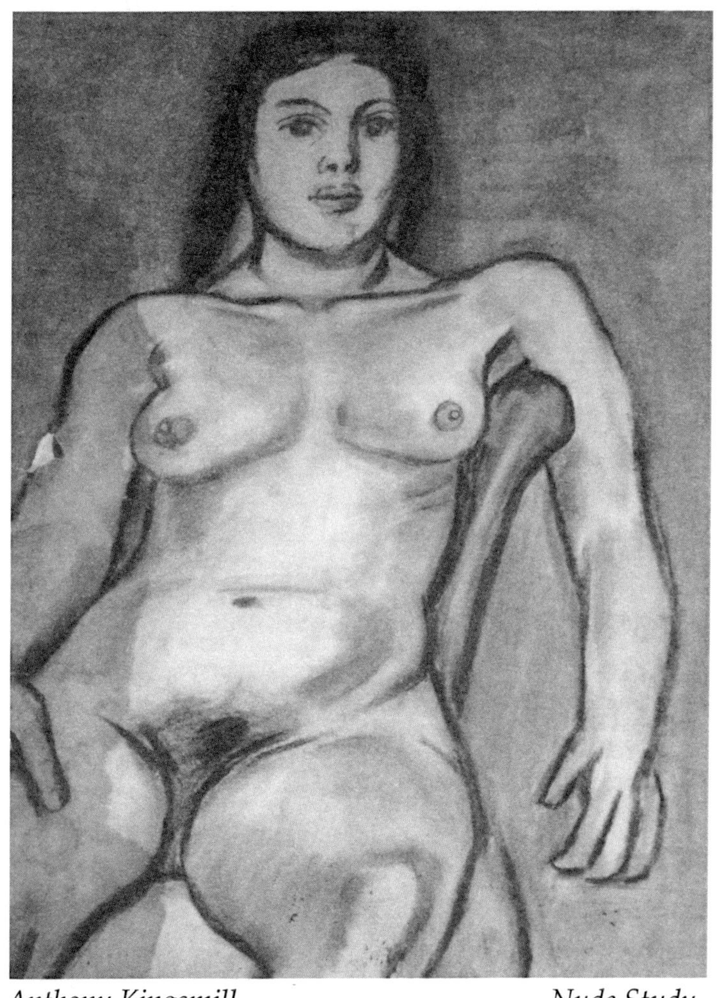

Anthony Kingsmill *Nude Study*

Seduction Of And By A Civilized Frenchwoman

Having agreed that Simone de Beauvoir's feminism is a bad joke
that Sartre is a has-been and a stupid
Jansenist muddleheaded
that Camus possessed more integrity than talent
that there are no longer any poets in France
worth mentioning
that much the same could be said for her novelists
and that, in general, French culture
is in a parlous condition, if not actually dead
not having to move
a single centimetre beyond Flaubert and Valery
and that no-one except the two of us
seemed to know what is happening in that wretched country
having agreed politely to disagree
about Hemingway, Rimbaud, Holderlin, Nietzche, Brecht, Lawrence, Moravia,
Jaspers, Kafka, Strindberg and Pasternak's Doctor Zhivago having dismissed politics as a betisse, religion as a folie
AND
Having inevitably but cautiously left the high ground

of literary and philosophical discussion
to speak of more personal, more mundane matters
i.e., one's dissatisfaction with conventional marriage, one's
adulteries, fornications, venereal diseases (there were none)
and a description of the circumstances attendant on one's best
and worst fucks
and having slightly dropped two or three hints
about one's favourite erogenous zones and best means to stimulate them
and having led from this to the over-riding , paramount need for tenderness,
mutual esteem, humour, delicatesse in sex and for similar though not identical tastes in literature, music, philosophy, art, theatre
and contemporary films
we are now ready to make love.

Anthony Kingsmill-Lunn
Hydra, May? 1987

How To Prepare A Canvas

for Imelda

1. Prepare Glue solution as follows:

a: Soak Glue in the water in which you are going to dissolve it the following day.

6 grms glue 100 grms water <u>Percentage 6%</u>

b: Disolue glue in bain-marie, not necessary that solution becomes too warm.

When solution is not too hot and not cold pass it over the stretched canvas lightly and try to cover well the whole surface.

Let then the canvas dry for 24 hours (flat on the floor)

2. Prepare sizing as follows:

a: Add a little water to the glue solution left over from the priming to replace the water that evaporated and heat again (bain-marie) the solution so that it becomes fluid.

b: Mix up in a pot an equal amount of zinc and chalk. This mixture must be approximately twice the amount of the glue solution you have nearby waiting (..for the killing).

Keep a little glue solution in a glass in case you may need it later.

The rest you pour it into the mixture of zinc and chalk. Very little at first, you mix as well as you can and then you pour the rest and you keep on mixing it till your arm starts aching. (then you run for the closest bench and you lie down for an hour or two).

If you see that the mixture is too thick (not really fluid) you add a little more glue solution (the one you had kept in the glass)

Pass the whole thing from a fine sieve once or twice.

c: with a large brush not too full you go over the canvas fairly fast. This first coat you scrape it then with the knife (before the seizing starts pulling) and you let it dry for about half to one hour.

d: You give the canvas then a second coat with the same mixture (Reheat it before this second coat, and add a little water to it) If you do not want the surface to even you scrape this coat too. This makes the canvas more elastic. Other wise you leave it and let it dry for 24 hours at least. Then you may consider yourself ready to produce a Rembrandt.

Love A.

Plain Brown Wrapper

To my astonishment he could cook.
Once, in the absence of his wife, produced
A creditable shepherd's pie
For the delectation of the two of us.

For starters, from a brown bag
Filled with flour, he plucked
An avocado - chef's tip
For ripening it.

His lifelong burden: "Grace"-
No hesitation, save mealtimes
Pronouncing it.

Once in a frigid restaurant I had urged
Him, shivering
To eat something to warm him up.

His caloric intake, so I presumed
Then, principally from drink. A pub
Ceiling where he had reproduced
Stag-hunts of Lascaux Caves- his culminating work
of art.

He had a knack, well-honed
For spotting someone's weak point, and dwelling on
It. Towards the end

Our last
Meal shared together - as banquet guests, I passed
Seconds - or was it thirds?
To him, companion to my left,

Of smoked salmon, thereby reducing him
To tears, owing in part
To his self-confessed
Fact, no food had passed his lips for ten days since.

Friend of George Barker, and others he identified
As "broken-hearted poets" he would recite
Them from memory, chapter and verse.

Till, council-housed pensioner
Fairly early on he took
Shelter beneath

That plain brown wrapper more associated with
Lazarus than dirty books.

"PLAIN BROWN RAPPER" by Ann Rivers
see also by Ann Rivers "A WORLD OF
DIFFERENCE" @Persephone Press

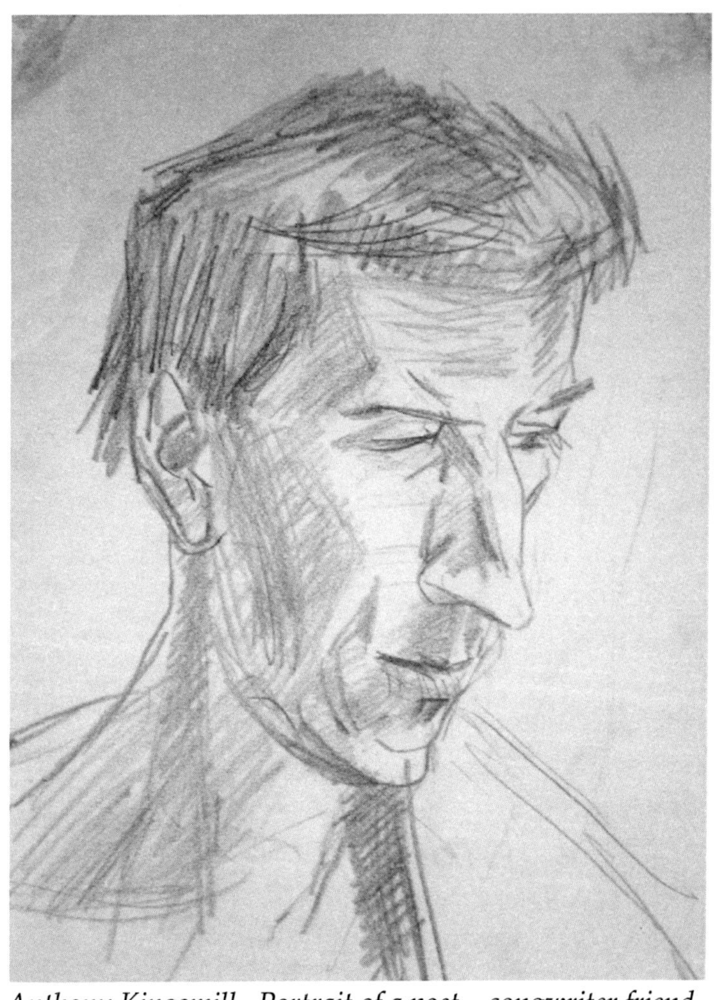

Anthony Kingsmill Portrait of a poet – songwriter friend

Dusko's Courtyard

In my fifty fathoms of night
you sway ah sway in lichen-lavender light
your iridescent your scented
your radiant hills
      anchor my dreams

In the breast oh in the pocket of winter
I keep your warm secret
of blue and whitewashed courtyards
bordered in perfume embroidered in grape
            in rose in jasmine

In the frozen   ah in the bitter air of exile
glitter of fig of olive of leaf
green-shimmer fish flashing the seas
            that ride my nights

In the empty   in the zero   in the snow
send   oh send me a pomegranate scorched
from your orchards
that I may bite
the sun

    Hydra, January 1986

for Ghika

Your ruined villa still
guards the broken hill
observing avarice and fire

It was a voice at dawn
that weeps for you
in this landscape of
hushed angelic blue
the sea and sky conspire

Its windows are blind
gutted eyes
focused on the new
painters who plague
your hill like locusts

Like some ancient stone
metronome it calmly counts
the figs which ripen and break
like these last days of August

 Hydra, 30 August 1986

Winter Island

for Anthony

Against the wind
the smoky sombas lit
In shuttered shops
the samovars steaming

Now the sullen sky   the cats
dreaming of fish   Now
the empty stones sulking
under the rain

Against the wind
the bulwark of our pain
All the hills streaming
with our tears

We remain
with the unused floats
fishing nets and firewood
stacked in the corners
of twilight cafes
hung with sausages and garlic
Outside
the gulls screaming

Sea – Change

for Imelda

Today the sea is a stranger
        wild and dark
on the stones
nets new-dyed in bark of pine
dry a deep brown like oak leaves

The wind's a knife
that pares all dullness
from the town
the light's new - hoped summer
has boarded the last ferry
and gone.

Anthony also has gone
but on your window's edge
the blue enamel pitcher
that held his brushes
glances with autumn light
catching all the lances
of the sun

 Hydra 28 August 1990
see also "The Poetry of Bettina Helen Massie"
@lulu.com

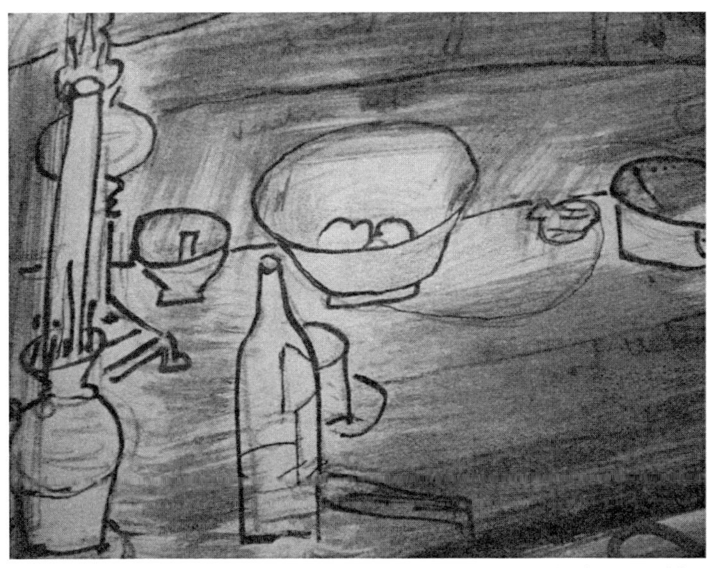

Anthony Kingsmill *Kitchen Table*

Stranded

Rock' n Roll has hit Ancient Greece
They' ve been around for quite a while
Rock' n Roll it's time for war
Off the ship to the Juke Box

dance around the olive trees
Women playing mister postman
Beach parties and fishermen
That's how romance was born

new music for Aegean lovers
Timeless wine in meat markets
Endless ouzo street corner confrontations
cafes, whores and drunken young men

another cigarette waiting for you
taking the boat to the lost island
fractured sunset of tears
bitching life of true arrogance
sharing our growing minds
subtle gestures silently suggesting the scene
the pain of separate togetherness
the only business of a soul mate

taking her to the circus
hearing the screams of the lonely, falling highwire artist
the teenage brunette's hair is mesmerising in the bright sun
glorious strands of red, blonde and orange

she walks through sponges and sandals
seeking a shocking change
the memory of the first kiss
the flaming movie of a haunted relationship

continuous scenes of fun and hate
burning coffee, spaghetti and Chablis
another evolution on horseback
another isolated exit and work

Alex Curzon Hale　　　　　　Hydra 1991

Hymn to Aphrodite

Oh yearning heart,
why does patience speak
and lay a hand upon your journey,
and when almost freed
to common things in this earth's treasure
then puts into your cup
a sparkle
weighed beyond the weight of measure...

Sweet strange music
plucked discordant,
lost
but for space between...

Love and beauty,
love
and beauty,
and naught else will stand its hymns of praise
and days past
which still emblazon the vision of nature...

It is not this man and woman now
no more than then,
the rhythm of pleasure
if one will sing again praise...
To the gods of Aphrodite

the choirs of Olympus rebound,
speak my yearning heart
to this sound…

Put flesh on your words
and worry no more
that else ought be found,
but to waken in the morning twilight
with your fellow creature,
bound as drops in the sea…

Richard Maelzel-Martins "The Seasons" Salzburg,
Austria 1968

see also by Richard Martins "THE THREE DAYS OF LOVE" @ Merlin Books.

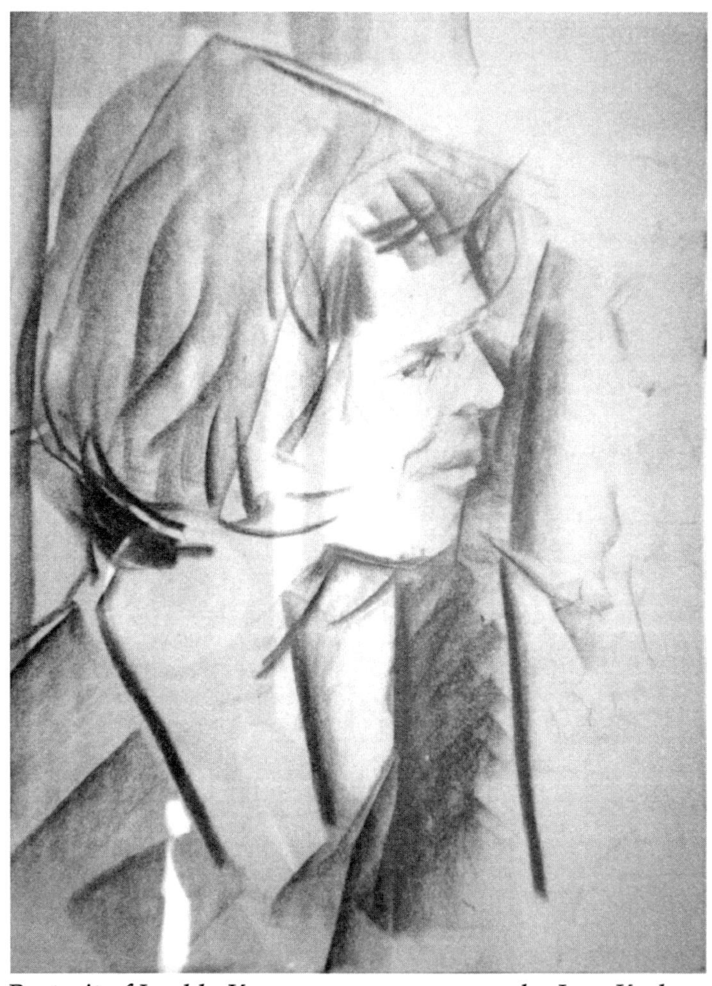

Portrait of Imelda Keyen *by Jens Karkov*

Incoherent Whispers

The day has finally come, it is November and raining in Brussels. Around the corner on the Avenue Louise is the office of Olympic Airways. How often when passing by have I looked at the columns of the Temple of Sounion braving the sky into a ray of blue unknown to this part of the world?

For the last time I descend the four flights of stairs, the door locking behind me with a dumped noise. The keys left in the letterbox clatter from the inside, and upon my face falls the first rain.

It feels light and refreshing.

A tram takes me past the pompous Palace of Justice, then the royal palace from where I can see the statue of Archangel Michael outlining the sky above the Grand Place.

The airport this morning is not busy, but a pleasant detachment kicks in and changes my autumn mood. How wonderful it is watching planes taking off nose up in the air through the clouds where indefinitely always the sun breaks through.

At the Olympic Airways counter I ask for a ticket to Athens, one way please. Cash in hand, it is handed over as if I was buying a sandwich with lettuce.

Boarding gate 22 at 11.30am.

Thank you.

The snow covered peaks of the Alps bathing in the bright sunlight lie beneath in majestic silence.

Athens in 1986, a noisy city full of life even in November.

I have been here before, on my way to Aegina to document a mosaic floor of an old Jewish synagogue.

The usual hustle and bustle of the taverns in the Plaka, the *rembetiko* musicians captivating me with their plaintive song, while I pick the olives out of my Greek salad.

Life is good.

A *kapheneion* near Omonia.

I am bending gloomily over a glass of white wine, crystal clear and chilled.

It must be refreshing in the summer I guess, but on this late evening it makes me feel cold.

An elderly man comes shivering in, carrying two huge plastic bags filled with packs of cigarettes. His being emits dullness and grey and mixes perfectly with the smoky cloud of the location. The difference between the cloud of smoke and his mass is a thin line.

Tired and clumsy, he staggers around the tables trying to sell cigarettes shouting

"Oriste tsigare, oriste.." while his voice gets lost among the empty chairs.

He crashes on one and orders a coffee.

Outside in the night the wind carries brown and orange pastel coloured leaves along on a soft breeze. Ladies in pink stroll by and turn their hips under the light of the lanterns.

The old man starts drawing over the condensation of the window glass, following with his finger the fall of the leaves.

Not one cigarette sold, the old man picks up his plastic bags and disappears, as a lost wolf, into the neon night.

A poetic symphony by Rachmaninov inspired by a painting by Bocklin, Hydra is the island of the Dead.

How many have died several deaths on Hydra to leave for another life? How many shedded old skin?

The Skull and Bones on Donkey lane weigh upon you before you start climbing up the steps.

The island of bliss where my neighbours Maria and Christos served me a glass of Dom Perignon champagne at Greek Easter, while roasting lamb in the spring sunshine surrounded by eucalyptus trees, wild flowers and the blue of the sea.

I found a small house for rent which was owned by the caretaker of the graveyard in Vlichos. From the terrace I could see the sea down in Kamini harbour.

Debussy's Clair de Lune and a warm fire were in sharp contrast with the tune of the deadsong of the church bells on a stormy January afternoon.

The old lady at Four Corners had died at four o'clock. It had been her favourite hour.

Beyond the scattering flames of a lazy fire I saw her again, sitting on the steps not far from Costa's mini market, surrounded by sleeping dogs in a hot summer sun. She was usually in full conversation with an invisible presence, a presence you came to accept because her wordy argument carried a no-nonsense reality. Maybe they both argued about the time and place of her final hours and couldn't agree, as her nervous gesturing and moaning discontent seemed to imply.

Sometimes the performance was interrupted when a passer-by tried to accelerate his step. Then she would lock you into a standstill with piercing eyes and ask for the time.

"Ti Hora ine??" Dutifully I always checked my watch and counted the hours out in Greek. Whatever the hour I mentioned, she did not blink.

Days passed and as none of my reported hours seemed to impress her, I decided to tell her the same time every time she asked before hurrying on.

This time being four o'clock.

From that day onwards I happily answered her question invariably with "it is four o'clock", *"ine tessera"*, which seemed to bring back a twinkle in her eyes and some life's content.

Her final question was solved, the deal was done.

The old lady had died on a Sunday afternoon, at four o'clock.

The woman offered him a cigarette out of her Camel brand pack. He took one, saying he did like the advertising outlay on the pack, the picture of the camel too but less.

I noticed that the picture on the pack depicted a dromedary with only one hump, and not a camel.

That summer all was not right.

The *meltemi* blew from the wrong direction and nerves were highly pitched.

The daily ritual however did not change.

Breakfast at Eva's, with Amstel beer for the addicts, followed by a stroll to the post office and shopping at the open market.

Then it was time for the first fashionable drink of the day, in the direction of "Up and High", overlooking the harbour with its shiny stone mansions and red roofs contrasting vividly with the blue of sky and sea.

Nina Simone in the background embraced you with her velvet voice when you entered this lovely place. Martinis, champagne, and the specially pressed fresh fruit juices set the pace for the daily problem to be solved: what shall we do and where shall we meet? The air seemed crowded with floating islands.

An attack on a cruise ship coloured the sky red, pink and lilac.

The sea protested and swallowed a Dutch tourist, while another one fell from a cliff.

A shark turned up draggling from Pan's boat one morning, keeping swimmers out of the water and sweating.

The tension built up when wildfires broke out on the island, causing fear of destruction and loss of life.

Finally everybody stayed in until Hydra's vibes had smoothed.

Watching a football match between Russia and Italy in "The Three Brothers" taverna became much more entertaining in the presence of German Wilhelm, Norwegian Felix and sweet Jimmy Parr, *tipota tiropita* and yes my dear!

High voltage in one room. The tables we occupied were as strategically placed as the Russian defence on the faraway field.

Wilhelm lived like an eagle high up in his eyrie on the top of the mountain, among cats and goats. The municipal garbage collected by donkeys never passed his way. He was too celestial for rubbish anyway, and had nothing to get rid of.

The water of the loo dripped from his windows when pulling the chain, so he said.

He seldom left his eagle's nest, and then only to come to the marketplace, and usually made it back home a couple of days later, after enjoying sunsets and sunrises in the available chairs at Tassos.

He was a painter who once trained in international law.

Jimmy Parr, sweet Jimmy was just Jimmy and appeared completely mad , *tipota tiropita* and yes my dear. He played his part well as mediator for the conversation between myself and Wilhelm. German Wilhelm rarely condescended into a conversation when not in the mood and the dialogue needed to be channelled through his pal Jimmy who happily obliged.

Another table was occupied by a Norwegian party, visiting Felix who lived on the island. Felix always staged an endless one man show waving eccentrically his long ebony cigarette holder, with or without a cigarette in, to accompany his incessant waterfall of words and opinions.

He had managed to fill his table with a great number of bottles of all sorts of beverage and sizes, so that the man sitting next to him could hardly reach for his food without knocking one over. They did not seem to have a great time.

The more his ebony cigarette holder waved through the air and his voice became louder, the more his table companion seemed discouraged and let his head sink towards the plate of fries in front of him.

The football score between Russia and Italy after twenty minutes was still 0-0.

I supported the Russians of course as a true Slavophile, but found myself the only one to do so.

Wilhelm at the other table groaned that it was a matter of fact that Americans did not understand what soccer was all about.

As if suddenly bitten by a snake or having received an injection of some kind, Felix got up and started to jump up and down, waving his arms with the extended ebony cigarette holder.. shouting in our direction if we did not know that his honourable family had endured bankruptcy after the first world war in the early twenties because of the Russians confiscating a great part of the Thoresen estate, and that they had remained broke ever since?

We did not know, but I imagined the confiscation of a huge iceberg with a polar bear on its top.

The Norwegian government having stripped all aristocratic titles, meant you could not address Felix by his title of count any longer. Instead you had to agree with several of his statements such as:

- the Norwegians discovered America before Columbus did, and left the native Indians in peace
- Viking mythology influenced Greek mythology
- Norwegians discovered Hydra

The man at his table started to sob. The effect of the wine had proved all too much.

Two ladies at the table started gently caressing his head.

At this point Felix lost his temper completely. He ordered them to leave on the grounds of their silly bourgeois behaviour, which they did without hesitation.

The man leaning between the two women, they stumbled out of the tavern.

The silence of the brotherhood returned.

Felix's head bobbed approvingly.

Suddenly a Russian goal in the Italian camp. 1-0.

They will come, the imperial eagles looking opposite ways but linked by their wings.

The unfathomable eyes of Petersburg, built on a swamp, preying on Europe.

Spreading out with the herds of Mongolia, the golden horde will arise.

Just a matter of time.

The woman sitting at the next table smoking Camels wears clothes of purple mud, puckering grenadine-painted lips as she pulls her cigarette. The wine makes her eyes roll from one corner into another.

We need more tulips and windmills.

Jimmy, dear Jimmy… do not despair when you are burning a candle for her each year, in the church.

That night in Brighton the sea was cold as she let her slim and frail body be taken by the waves. The wind does not play in her hair.

The salty sea swallows a butterfly and a night bat screams.

The stars shiver terrified while rain falls softly in the sand.

Imelda Keyen Hydra 1987

Prophitis Elias

Through the swirling mountain mist we slowly climb,
Glancing at the receding blue deep and going back in time.
There are ants to dodge and rude walking sticks to find
Finally the old gates and walls enfold us, bring peace to mind
Whoa! The furry mascot has appeared from the door of a cell
And he is bounding around the wide courtyard, bidding us farewell

Donald Macleod 2008

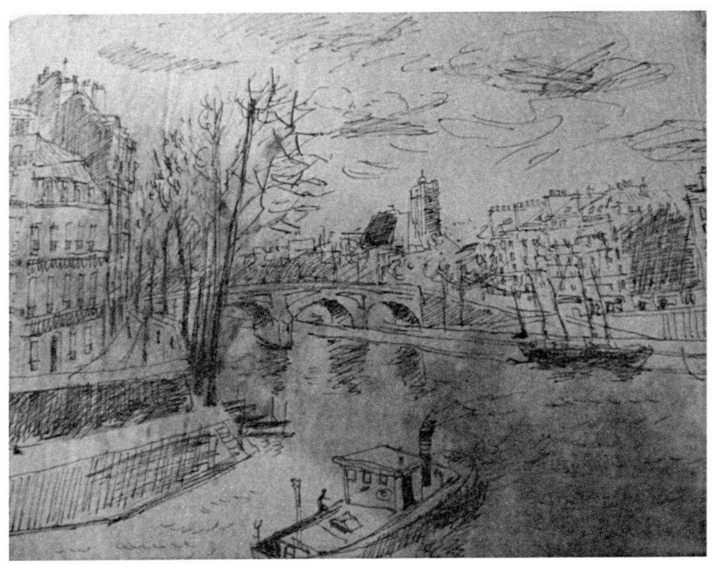

Anthony Kingsmill *Paris in the Spring 1952*

Time of thyme

Among the high rocks and occasional trees
we plod steadily through the sea breeze
then tiptoe across the island's sleeping backbone
to gaze on the deep sea guarding Minos' throne.
Before long the lowering cloud bids us return
on the long path back our poor feet will burn
but as lovers we smell and gather the thyme
with which we can concoct a kitchen rhyme.

Donald Macleod 2009

Maria

Amid the rocks of Kamini village
nestling behind the old church
lived the old guardian of the steps.
Known to all, held in awe by a few.
From her one window songs echoed
to summon the cats to drink
and jostle the drunken sailor.
After Mayday hubbub all will be quiet

In memory of Maria Tsitinakis.
Donald Macleod July 2009

Passing through Piraeus

Through efficient and pristine ways
we are delivered to the port where
under the old clock (non-existing) we are
fully recharged and recognise each other
once more as two xenophobes-in-arms
headed to our home from home where
all is present and correct and none disturbs

Donald Macleod October 2010

Peace

No cantankerous neighhbours here (yet),
only the clip clop of hooves and the
occasional cry of a child under the
blue sky later to become a starry field.
A short walk takes us to the sea's breath
Never ceasing and always inspiring.
Our bed encompasses the whole island

Donald Macleod October 2010